A Labyrinth Pilgrimage

A Pilgrim Journey to the Foot of the Cross
Revised

C. A. Radke

A Labyrinth Pilgrimage
A Pilgrim Journey to the Foot of the Cross
Revised

Visit
http://www.CrossLabyrinth.com
for finger labyrinths
and additional copies of this book.

Table of Contents

Acknowledgements

First and foremost and always, I acknowledge God, who from eternity to eternity is gracious, merciful, and full of loving kindness; Jesus Christ, the Word made flesh, who dwelt among us, full of grace and truth; and the Holy Spirit, the Comforter and the gift of the Father by which we are baptized.

My wife, Nanette, is the very reflection of God's love. The contribution of her encouragement and support cannot be overstated. I will never be able to thank her adequately, though I certainly shall try all my life long.

I would be remiss if I failed to acknowledge Rev. John D. Smith of Hawthorn, South Australia, who, though we have never met face to face, has been a dear, dear brother in Christ for several years. John, you have been steadfast, and a very genuine inspiration to me. I pray that I will continue learning to follow the example of authentic faith that I have come to see in you.

Finally, I have known Christian encouragement from people in my work and in my worship. I thank you all, and I give thanks to God for you.

Introduction

There are many labyrinth designs, and many books and publications about using labyrinths. This book is an aid for taking a labyrinth pilgrimage during the season of Lent using the Cross Labyrinth, which I designed especially for use in Christian spiritual formation. In addition to its portrayal of the cross, the best known symbol of Christianity, this labyrinth has a natural connection with Lent. The Lenten season consists of forty days, not including Sundays. If each Sunday during Lent and Easter Sunday are added, the total time is forty-seven days, which corresponds with the forty-seven straight lines found in the Cross Labyrinth. This book contains a devotion for each day of that journey.

To introduce the reader to the labyrinth as a tool for prayer and meditation, this introduction provides a brief guide to use the Cross Labyrinth for a personal pilgrimage.

The Cross Labyrinth
Like many of the smaller classical labyrinths, the Cross Labyrinth has a seven-circuit path. Seven is a significant number in scriptures, from the seven-day account of creation in Genesis to the imagery that revolves around the number seven in the book of Revelation. It is a number of completion. When a pilgrim has completed seven circuits in the Cross Labyrinth, the journey to the cross is complete.

Seven is also a number of wholeness or "one-ness." Three is a number associated with God, and four is associated with the Earth or creation. The sum of the two numbers is seven, and represents the Creator at one with creation.

In the Cross Labyrinth, four circuits lie inside the arms of the cross and represent creation in need of salvation. The other three circuits surround the cross, and represent God's presence always surrounding us.

The perimeter of the cross itself is not considered a circuit, but tracing the cross will provide an eighth path. Eight is a number of resurrection or renewal (Christ arose on the eighth day), and 888 is the number of Christ.

Pilgrimage
For Christians, pilgrimage is an ancient tradition dating back at least to the 4th century A.D. The earliest pilgrim journeys visited the Holy Land, going to the places where Christ Himself lived and walked and performed His earthly ministry. Pilgrims withdrew from their day to day lives. Leaving all of their worldly ambitions and concerns behind them, they visited places such as Bethlehem, Nazareth, the Sea of Galilee, Jerusalem, Calvary, and surrounding areas. They were driven by their sincere commitment to Christ, and by their thirst to deepen their faith. Their time was focused on their Lord. Their minds were focused on their Lord. Their hearts were focused on their Lord. When they arrived at their destination, they were prepared to encounter Christ in a new and special way. Everything that they had and everything that they did revolved so completely around their devotion to God that they could not help being changed. A pilgrimage was not complete, though, until the return journey. The return would retrace the journey back to its origin. Pilgrims returned to the same communities they had left, but they returned as changed people.

Labyrinth Pilgrimage
The labyrinth is used as a pilgrimage. Like the early pilgrimages, following the labyrinth represents a journey.

It is not a journey to the Holy Land, but it is a journey to a holy place. It is a journey that leaves day to day life behind. It is a journey that sets aside all ambitions and concerns. It is a journey to that place where God's people worship in spirit and in truth; a journey of sincere commitment to Christ; a journey to a deeper faith. Pilgrims' time in the labyrinth should be focused on Christ. Their minds should be focused on Christ. Their hearts should be focused on Christ. The journey into the labyrinth can prepare pilgrims to encounter Christ in a new and special way—a life changing way. After communing with God, pilgrims return. They retrace the path, returning to where they began, but returning as changed people.

Walking a Labyrinth
The Cross Labyrinth is not a maze. It is a path. It has no wrong turns. It leads from the entrance to one place. In the Cross Labyrinth, that place is the foot of the cross.

As you trace the path to the cross, remember that this is a journey. It is a pilgrimage. Breathe deeply and leave the ambitions and concerns of daily life behind. Expect to encounter Christ. Open yourself to a deeper relationship. Focus this time on Christ. Focus your mind on Christ. Focus your heart on Christ.

As you move along the path you might say a familiar prayer or a "breath prayer" silently, perhaps quietly aloud. You might turn your thoughts to the words of a hymn such as "Turn Your Eyes upon Jesus," or "When I Survey the Wondrous Cross." Feel the excitement welling up inside of you as the path leads you closer to the cross. Feel the yearning as the path takes you farther away. Think of the nails that pierced Christ as you pass the hands and feet of the cross. Remember the spear that ripped through His side.

At the same time, consider where you are in relation to the cross—beside the cross, above the cross, beneath the cross—but not quite "at" the cross.

Finally the path will lead to the foot of the cross. Pause there and reflect.
- For you, Christ came to earth.
- For you, Christ fulfilled prophecy.
- For you, Christ suffered on the cross.
- For you, Christ died.
- For you, Christ lay in the tomb.
- For you, Christ arose victorious.
- For you, Christ ascended.
- For you, Christ will return.

Remember the soldiers who cast lots for Jesus' garments at the foot of the cross. If you could, would you seek a chance to "win" His clothes? If Christ offered to clothe you, what garment would you take? What would it symbolize to you?

Take time to trace the perimeter of the cross. You are touching it just at the edge. If you are so moved, run your finger over the surface of the cross and remember that Jesus suffered there for you.

As you pass the first hand, consider your place next to Christ. Are you like one of the thieves? Which one? Consider yourself on his cross.

As you pass the head, consider the crown that Christ wore. Think about the sign that was posted. What sign would you put at the head of Jesus' cross?

As you pass the other hand, consider the other thief. Consider yourself on his cross. What would you say to Jesus?

As you are returning to the foot of the cross, consider the soldier who pierced Christ to the heart. He used his spear to make certain that Jesus was dead, but in doing so he encountered Christ in such a powerful way that he was compelled to confess that truly, Christ is the Son of God.

Take as much or as little time as you need to pray and meditate, or to simply sit in silence. Then take time to retrace the path back to the beginning. Like the early pilgrims who traveled to Israel, return to the world you came from. The world will not be any different, but you will be.

Having taken a brief journey, let's begin a pilgrimage together.

Creation

This week focuses on the Genesis account of creation. Because our journey begins on Ash Wednesday, this will be the shortest week of our pilgrim journey. Each week of Lent will lead to a Sunday during Lent, and the final week of Lent will lead to the triumph and celebration of Easter.

In the Beginning

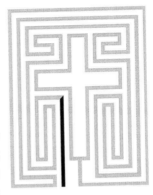

In the beginning God created the heaven and the earth. Genesis 1:1

It is the first day of our journey. We leave behind the things that are familiar to us. We know about these things based on what we have seen and experienced through our senses. But where did it all come from? What does it all mean?

It is hardly any wonder that the writers of the scriptures had the same questions. Thousands of years before Christ, before the Christian Era, the first verse of the first chapter of the first book of the Bible began by recounting the actions of God before there was any written record; before there were any people; before there was anything. There was nothing to see. Nothing to hear. Nothing to touch. Nothing. Nothing at all. The writer begins at "the beginning"–before anything else happened.

Who was there? God, and God alone.

Pause and think of it. God alone. Close your eyes. Take a deep breath. When you enter the labyrinth, leave creation behind. You are starting a journey to encounter God, and God alone. If you experience a sense of awe, good! A sense of exhilaration, better! A sense of love–you have found the first step of your pilgrimage.

The Psalmist knew the same sense of awe.

Before the mountains were brought forth, or ever you formed the earth and the world, even from everlasting to everlasting, you are God. Psalm 90:2

The sea is his, and he made it: and his hands formed the dry land. Psalm 95:5

The sea, the land, and the mountains. All of them were formed by God. And so were you.

I praise you because I am fearfully and wonderfully made; your works are wonderful, I know that full well. Psalm 139:14

For this pilgrimage, leave the world behind. Set God before you. God, and God alone.

Dearest God, creator of heaven and earth, creator of life and creator of my soul, you are truly awesome. I tremble at your greatness, and I am humbled. I am at the beginning of a journey. I am seeking you. I am seeking you alone. Watch over me. Keep me ever in your loving care, and reveal yourself to me, that I may be a faithful witness to your everlasting power and love. Amen.

Days of Creation

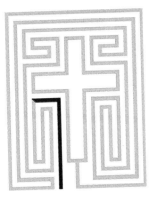

"And the evening and the morning were the first day." Genesis 1:5b

The creation account in Genesis 1 reflects the orderly character of God. Each day new things were created. Each step in the creation sequence prepared the way for things to come. Heaven and earth were created on the first day. Without them, where could the rest of creation occur? Light was also created on the first day. Light is an essential source of energy for the rest of creation, and it is also an inspiring symbol of the nature of God. On the second day He divided the waters, followed by the creation of land and plants on the third. This is also orderly and logical. Without light and water plants could not grow. The same cycle was repeated for animals and humans in the next three days, with lights on the fourth day, creation of animals in the waters on the fifth, and creation of animals on the land on the sixth. On the sixth day, having prepared everything else, God also created man. When He had completed this work, God rested on the seventh day.

A pilgrimage is also an orderly process, and pilgrims depend on light, water, and plants. Light is essential to see the path. Water and nourishment are needed to give life and strength. As in the creation story, the cycles of light, water, and nourishment repeat during the pilgrimage, and each cycle prepares us for the path ahead.

On a pilgrimage, the need for order and preparation is not limited to the physical journey. It is even more important for the spiritual journey. From Old Testament times, people have been called to prepare themselves to encounter and serve God. Samuel told the Israelites, "Prepare your hearts unto the LORD, and serve him only: and he will deliver you."

The symbols of light, water, and nourishment have powerful meaning on a spiritual pilgrimage. Spiritual light gives us inspiration and vision. Christ said, "I am come a light into the world, that whoever believes on me should not abide in darkness." John 12: 46. Spiritual water gives life and quenches the yearnings of the soul. Jesus said to the woman at the well, "Whoever drinks of the water that I shall give him shall never thirst; but the water that I shall give him shall be in him a well of water springing up into everlasting life." John 4:14. Spiritual food satisfies our hunger and gives us strength for the journey. Speaking to the people who followed Him after the miracle of fishes and loaves our Lord said, "I am the bread of life: he that comes to me shall never hunger." John 6:35.

On this pilgrimage, let Jesus be your light. Let Him quench the thirsting of your soul. Let him satisfy the hunger of your spirit.

Great and awesome Creator God, your order is in everything that I see. It is Your light that lets me see, Your water that quenches my thirst, Your food that sustains me. You are my all in all. Guide me on my journey with Your light. Refresh my soul with Your water of eternal life. Nourish my spirit with Your food, the bread of heaven. In all of creation around me, remind me always of Your order and Your plan to provide. I am grateful. For everything I am grateful. In the name of Your Son, Jesus the Christ, my light, my water, and my bread of life, Amen.

Poetry of Creation

These are the generations of the heavens and of the earth when they were created, in the day that the LORD God made the earth and the heavens. Genesis 2:4

God's creation is not merely the product of an orderly process. It is beautiful, intriguing, and diverse. The earth is filled with rich colors and subtle hues; roaring rivers and whispering breezes; majestic mountains and secret ocean depths. Plants of every size and shape are abundant, and each is fitted to the environment that God prepared for it. The variety of animal life is equally breath taking, from microscopic creatures to immense denizens of land and sea. The heavens are filled with beauty and mystery too great to describe. Truly, creation is a reflection of God's imagination. It is a gallery of God's art. It is a symphony of unsurpassable power and beauty.

In contrast with the structured, daily progression described in Genesis 1, the account of creation in Genesis 2 captures a sense of God's artistry. The words flow like those of a master story teller or a poet. They are designed to move the listener back in time. Back, before there were plants. Back, before there was rain. Back, before the time of man. Having cleared the canvas, the poet begins to weave a love story. It is the story about God's love for mankind; a story about our needs; a story about our purpose; a story about our companionship and relationship with both the Creator and the creation. It is inspired and it is inspiring. If you have never done it before, take time to read aloud Genesis 2:4-25.

Pilgrimage is a journey to know more about God and encounter Him in a new way. It leaves the cares and distractions of the world behind. Even so, take time to marvel at God's handiwork. We know God better when we see what He has done and what He is doing. Creation is an expression of who God is and how much He loves us. It is His sculpture, His sonnet, His creation. And we are a part of it.

Great God, creator and lover of my soul, I marvel at the work of Your hands. Heaven and earth are filled with Your glory, and Your glory surrounds me. Thank you for the beauty of creation. Thank you for Your boundless love, a love that bids me walk with You and gives me strength and joy and companionship. Lead me always in this path of beauty and love, and throughout my life inspire me to share Your glory and Your ways with all those around me. Amen.

It was good

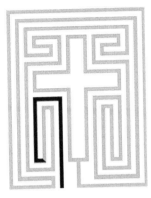

God saw all that he had made, and, behold, it was very good.
Genesis 1:31a

Before we go too far on our pilgrim journey, there is another important lesson to take from the creation stories. While God was working, He was also evaluating what He had done. Step by step and day by day, God looked at what He had done and saw that it was good. At the end of the process, He looked at everything and saw that it was very good.

Although the Creator provided us with His own example of doing good work and building on it, we have a tendency to pursue a different course. Consider the example of King David. One evening he saw a beautiful woman washing herself. He asked about her and learned that she was married. David could have considered his situation and left her alone, but he chose to send for her. David could have sent her home, but he chose to have an affair and she became pregnant. David could have sought forgiveness from her and her husband, but he chose to arrange the man's death. Instead of following God's example by confirming that each step was good, David made things worse with every decision he made. His choices planted seeds that separated him from God, violated a woman, killed a man, wounded his family, and eventually divided a nation. Even though David would later repent, damage had been done which could not be undone.

We have the opportunity to grow as followers of Christ by evaluating our progress on this journey. We have only been on our pilgrimage for a few days, but it is not too early to consider whether the path we are following is a good path or something less. Are our motives pure? Are our hearts humble? Are we truly preparing ourselves for a journey with God?

If today's steps were good, then we have something good to build upon. If today's steps were not good, now is the time to make a change. It is not enough to do better than David. God set the standard at creation. Every step must be a good step. Every day must be a good day. We should strive to follow God's example so that each step is good, and the final result is very good.

Most perfect Father in heaven, thank you for Your wondrous creation. It is good. It is very good. Thank you for showing me the importance of doing things well step by step and day by day. Give me the wisdom, the patience, and the courage to review my work and my behavior honestly and fairly so that I can build upon that which is good. Let every word from my mouth and every work of my hands bring glory and honor to You. Amen.

Walking with God

And the LORD God formed man of the dust of the ground, and breathed into his nostrils the breath of life; and man became a living soul. Genesis 2:7

The first Easter happened on the first day of the week, a Sunday. In a sense, every Sunday is a miniature Easter celebration. Every Sunday, Christians gather to celebrate the resurrection of Jesus and His undeniable victory over sin and death. Christ laid down his pure and righteous life by giving it up on the cross. But the cross could not hold Him. Death held no power over Him. He arose, and He walked among us!

The power to give life comes from God alone. Every time that God gives life, it is an act of love and an invitation to walk together in a relationship filled with purpose and joy. God filled Adam with the breath of life at creation, and Adam walked with God. God revived the body of Jesus on Easter, and God walked with us.

Today is the first Sunday during Lent. Even though Sundays are not counted in the forty days of Lent, we are still on our pilgrim journey. We are still seeking an intimate, personal encounter with God. We are still seeking to walk with Him so that we can have a relationship filled with purpose and joy.

Remember that God gave us life so that we can walk with Him. Remember that Christ arose so that He could walk with us. What a precious invitation to walk together!

God of life and God of breath, you alone are God. You alone give life. You alone are life. Thank you for the life you have given me. Thank you for the lives of those around me. Let me praise you for your greatness. Give me purpose and give me joy in this journey. Let me walk with You, as You walk with me. In the name of Jesus Christ, my risen Lord, Amen.

Separation

Devotions this week focus on man's fall from perfect fellowship with God. Each week through Palm Sunday will end with a devotion focused on peace in promise, as God began His great work of salvation for a fallen world.

The Attraction of Creation

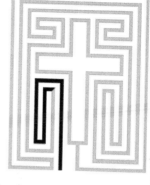

And out of the ground made the LORD God to grow every tree that is pleasant to the sight, and good for food. Genesis 2:9a

God made trees that are beautiful to see. They bear fruit that is wonderful to eat. As God created the world, He looked at everything He made and called it good. This was no accident. He did it on purpose. Creation was supposed to be good. It was supposed to be useful. It was supposed to be attractive: a perfect place for a perfect relationship between God and His people.

The attraction of creation is just as strong today as it ever was. Consider the majestic grandeur of snow-capped mountain ranges. Think about the awesome power of ocean waves as they crash along the beach. Beautiful wild flowers blooming in the fields, graceful eagles soaring across the skies, slender palms swaying in the wind—all of them are the handiwork of God. All of them have existed since creation, and all of them continue to inspire us.

Creation is more than mountains and oceans and plants and animals. Consider a mother and child laughing as they play in a grassy field, or a boy and girl holding hands on their first date. The bonds of love and friendship are the fruit of God's hand, and they are wonderfully attractive, too.

Creation exists at God's pleasure and for our enjoyment. It is good for us to admire and enjoy it. On this pilgrim journey, look at all that God has done and give thanks.

Enjoyment should be coupled with a spirit of humble gratitude. We do not enjoy creation due to anything we have done or earned, but because of the abundant love of the Creator.

Gracious God and giver of all good things, what a glorious world You have made. I see the works of Your hands and marvel. It is too much for me to understand. Thank you for Your bountiful provision. Thank you for Your steadfast love. Be always with me on my journey today. Amen.

The Forbidden Fruit

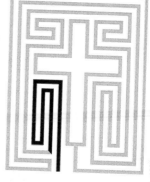

But of the tree of the knowledge of good and evil, you shall not eat of it: for in the day that you eat thereof you shall surely die.
Genesis 2:17

So far on our pilgrimage we have focused on things that are good, but there is more to know. God prepared the earth for people and we are supposed to enjoy it, but God also created some things that are not for us at all.

Genesis says that God placed many trees in the Garden of Eden and told Adam to take care of them. Adam was welcome to eat from any tree except for one—the tree of the knowledge of good and evil. This tree belonged in the garden because God put it there, but that did not mean that Adam was welcome to it. Instead, God told Adam to leave it alone. God also told Adam what would happen if he disobeyed.

The Garden of Eden is gone today. The tree of the knowledge of good and evil is gone with it. No one alive today has seen them, and we will never see them again. Even so, they are far more than historical curiosities. They are still relevant to us in everything we do.

Like God's original relationship with Adam in the Garden, God still wants us to find Him in a perfect place where we can experience a perfect relationship. Jesus spoke about it 2,000 years ago. Talking with a Samaritan woman He said, "But the hour comes, and now is, when the true worshippers shall worship the Father in spirit and in truth: for the Father seeks such to worship him." God wants us to worship Him—He seeks us to worship Him! The pilgrimage that we are on now is part of our life's journey to worship God in spirit and in truth.

As with the tree of the knowledge of good and evil at creation, God created some things that are not intended for our use or consumption today. There are rules and limits, and our relationship with God depends in part on how we deal with those limits. God tells us what they are, and He tells us what will happen if we break His rules.

As we continue on our pilgrimage and live from day to day, we should remember that God desires a perfect relationship with us. He wants to meet us in a perfect place. He seeks people who worship Him in spirit and in truth. Remember that God has rules to bless us and keep us safe. God blesses us with His love. We honor God through humble obedience.

Holy God, I adore you. I exalt your name. I seek to worship you. Your creation is glorious, and your rules are righteous. Teach me to worship you in spirit and in truth. Write on my heart the rules that must guide me, and teach me the joy of humble obedience. All this I ask in the name of Jesus, Son of God and son of man, Amen.

The Mysterious and Beguiling Creature

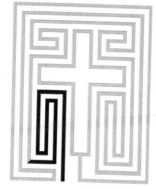

Now the serpent was more subtle than any beast of the field which the LORD God had made.
Genesis 3:1a

There is a sensation that we experience when we encounter the unknown. It is very difficult to describe. Perhaps this is because there are no words to describe this sensation. Perhaps it is because the sensation itself is part of the unknown. Whatever the reason may be, whether we can describe it or not, it is a real sensation. It is almost tangible.

The account of Eve and the serpent evokes that sensation. Although we don't know exactly what it looked like, we can picture the serpent suspended in the branches of a lovely tree—the tree of the knowledge of good and evil. The creature is almost imperceptible, but then it moves and its patterned skin draws our eyes along its body, winding this way and that, finding its way to a flat, dark-eyed head. Its stare is simultaneously repulsive and intriguing. It moves again and passes by a piece of fruit—the forbidden fruit! Without speaking a word, the serpent is taunting us. It beguiles us. It is in the tree that man cannot touch. It caresses the fruit that man cannot eat. The fruit is lovely and inviting. The fruit is distracting. Of all the good things that God created, this is the one that we cannot have.

A similar yet different sensation is evoked when we enter into a holy place. On this pilgrimage we seek to encounter

God in a new way. Because it is new, it involves an encounter with the unknown. The similarity with the feeling evoked by the mysterious and beguiling creature in the Garden of Eden is undeniable, but the difference is just as real. What is the difference? How do we know which sensation is good, and which one is not?

The Psalmist struggled with the same questions. In one psalm he decries the wicked people who lay in secret, waiting for their victims; in another psalm he takes refuge in the secret place of the most High. Both the wicked and the holy have their mysteries and secrets, but they are not the same. The secrets of the wicked lead to disobedience, destruction, and death; the secret ways of the Lord lead to comfort, blessing, and life eternal.

On this pilgrim journey and throughout our lives we will encounter the unfamiliar and the unknown. We do not have to be confused about our choices, though. As lovely and enticing as the wrong choice may seem, it will always involve an element of disobedience or self interest. In contrast, the way of righteousness always involves humble, selfless obedience to God. In case we lose our direction, we can remember where we are going. Our journey leads to the foot of the cross, the symbol of Christ's humble, selfless obedience. It is the symbol that leads to resurrection and life.

Holy, righteous, almighty God, I have no words to describe my awe and wonder. I sense your holiness and I feel unworthy. I am enticed by desires that distract me from your path and lead me to disobey your words. Create in me a clean heart, O God, a heart that is hungry for your Word and a will that is ever conformed to your ways. This I pray in the name of Christ, my Lord, Amen.

In Spite of All Warning

Of the fruit of the tree which is in the midst of the garden, God has said, "You shall not eat of it, neither shall you touch it, lest you die." Genesis 3:3

Everyone encounters difficulty or danger from time to time. Sometimes danger takes us by surprise. Most of the time, though, plenty of information is available, and there are many signs and warnings in advance. Consider driving a car from one town to another. Some information is painted on the road itself, including dashed lines to mark the lanes and solid lines to mark "no passing" zones. Signs are posted beside the road with information like speed limits, school zones, intersections, and steep road grades. Barricades are placed to prevent us from driving into dangerous conditions. If there is flooding or other danger, traffic officers may be stationed to monitor the situation and give warnings directly to each driver.

We have to make decisions when we receive information. We avoid collisions by staying inside the lines. We take extra care driving through school zones and over steep grades. We stop at barricades to avoid hazards. We follow the directions of traffic officers because we know that they are there to keep us safe. In spite of all of this information, though, we still have accidents. We still experience injury. And most of the time, it is because someone did not follow the rules and did not heed the warnings.

In the Garden of Eden, God provided Adam and Eve all of the signs that they needed. He warned them personally. If there was any question about it, Eve quoted God's warning when she spoke with the serpent. In spite of all warning, though, they crossed the line. They crashed the barriers. They embraced danger instead of love. They found themselves separated from their Maker.

Before we judge them too harshly, though, we have to step back. What lines do we cross? What barriers do we crash? What warnings do we ignore?

We are on a journey to encounter God. God's lines are straight. His signs are clear. His barriers protect us. His warnings are for our safety. In God's safety, we find His love. Danger on a spiritual journey is not exciting. It is only dangerous. We should embrace God's love.

God, I know that you love me. I know that you only seek to bless me. Give me eyes to see your signs. Give me wisdom to follow your way. When I am tempted to throw caution to the wind and bare my soul to the perils of sin, warn me again. Give me the humility and courage to heed your words, for I know that in your paths my soul is safe. In Jesus' name I pray, Amen.

Together in Hiding, But All Alone

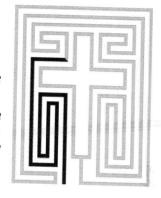

And they heard the voice of the LORD God walking in the garden in the cool of the day: and Adam and his wife hid themselves from the presence of the LORD God amongst the trees of the garden. Genesis 3:8

We may never fully understand what it is about human nature that leads us to break rules, challenge authority, and rebel. Even more curious, though, is the way that we often behave after we act out. We brashly do what we never should have done, and then we cover up. We hide. We deny. We make excuses. We try to blend into the crowd, but at the same time we make sure that we stay separated from the crowd. After all, we can't trust "them."

The sad truth is that we have been doing this since the beginning of human history. Adam and Eve ate the forbidden fruit. Then Adam started the first phase. "Quick, Eve, cover your body." Eve continued, "Uh oh, Adam, *He's* coming! Hide. NOW!" Typical human response. Covering up, hiding, and trying to avoid the only one who really loved them.

After a little more of this proved futile, Adam began phase two. "God, are you asking about fruit? Oh—you mean *that* fruit? Well, you know you set me up with *her*, and now see what *she* did." Eve chimed right in. "Me? Hey, I was tricked by the snake." Typical again. Denial. Excuses. Lying to themselves and lying to God.

Notice what happened. While they were pushing God away, they began to push away from each other, too. What they didn't realize is that separation is not what they needed. They needed to face God. They needed to confess and seek forgiveness and reconciliation.

We are prone to the same behavior today. Who do we hide from? We hide from God. We hide from spouses, managers, and friends. If anyone gets close enough to see our faults, we push them away. We deny fault. We make excuses. Like Adam and Eve, this is not what we need. We need confession. We need forgiveness. We need reconciliation.

On our journey, we have to remember that we cannot draw close to God while we push Him away. We cannot grow in His family while we alienate our brothers and sisters. When we are wrong, we need to confess. When we are hurt, we need to forgive. When we grow apart, we need to reconcile. As we continue our pilgrimage to encounter God, be sure to draw closer to God. Don't push Him away.

Holy God, you are the one God. You are my all in all. I desire to be one with you and one with your people. Even though I sin, Lord, let me seek your face. Let me confess my faults. Let me reconcile to you. Give me a heart like your heart, Lord, that I may love your children, even as you do. This I ask in your holy name, Amen.

Cast Out, but Never Abandoned

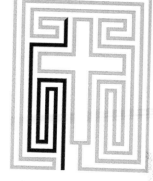

Therefore the LORD God sent him forth from the garden of Eden, to till the ground from whence he was taken. Genesis 3:23

A precious relationship can be compared with a piece of fine jewelry. Fine jewelry is crafted with greatest care from the finest materials. It is polished to capture every sparkle, and when it is finished it is displayed as the centerpiece. It commands the highest price, and it is kept as a priceless treasure. Even when it is put away, it is protected and valued and cared for.

A relationship is a beautiful and wondrous thing, too. It is cultivated carefully from a foundation of love. It is nurtured to embrace every facet, and when it is seen it captures everyone's attention. It receives our best attention, and is protected tenderly. When there is distance or separation, it is still in the heart and on the mind.

The most precious relationship that we have is our relationship with God. It was developed in love and from love. It was nurtured in perfection and given the central role in all of creation.

When Adam and Eve sinned, they created distance in their relationship with God. They tried to hide themselves from God, and God sent them out of the Garden of Eden. Even so, God never abandoned them. He continued to treat the relationship as a treasure. Adam had to till the soil for food, but even that provided an important message. God was telling the people to work and live. God never told them that He didn't want to hear from them any more. They were still loved. They were still precious.

We are created for a relationship with God, too. Sometimes we sin and we create distance in our relationship. Our unholiness cannot remain in God's presence, but He never abandons us. He still loves us and seeks our return. Jesus told us that heaven rejoices when sinners repent. God never forgets us at all.

If you stumble on your pilgrim journey, don't give up—just get up. God won't give up on you. He will not abandon you. The love is still there. The love is still there for you.

O loving God, your love is deeper than I can comprehend. Even though I disobey you and sin against you, your love is steadfast. No matter how I hide, you still seek me. No matter where I go, you never abandon me. Thank you for your infinite love. Teach me to repent from my sin so that the heavens will rejoice, and lead me in your ways so that all the world will glorify you. In the name of your son, Jesus, Amen.

Peace in Promise

I will put enmity between you and the woman, and between your seed and her seed; he shall bruise your head, and you shall bruise his heel. Genesis 3:15

The promises of God do not fail us. Even when we fail, God is good. Adam and Eve failed to honor God's direction for their lives. They suffered the consequences, but God still loved them and cared for them. Generation after generation we have all failed to honor God, but He is still good.

In the garden, God told the serpent that there would be enmity between the tempter and mankind throughout time. In the fullness of time, though, Christ fulfilled the early prophecy of Genesis 3:15. Although Satan was able to inflict pain on Christ in His humanity, Christ was victorious. Satan was relegated to nothing more than a serpent that was trodden under foot.

Christ is greater than any other person. He alone is the Christ, the Messiah, the Son of the living God. His victory was foretold. We can know peace because this is the Christian era, and so it shall remain because Christ lives and reigns, and He shall return.

Blessed God, thank you for your love and for your promises. I praise you that, although Satan has the power to wound us, you have provided the way to overcome. Let me live in your peace because of your promises. Amen.

The Human Condition

Devotions this week focus on ways that people honor God, as well as some of the ways that we create problems by alienating ourselves from God and our neighbors.

Honoring God in His Way

And Abel, he also brought of the firstlings of his flock and of the fat thereof. And the LORD had respect unto Abel and to his offering. Genesis 4:4

There are so many different aspects of giving. We can consider the kinds of things that are given, their value, the timing, and the setting. There are intangible aspects, too. Some people say it is the thought that counts. The scriptures reflect God's reactions to gifts and offerings. Those accounts tell us everything that we really need to know.

The earliest accounts of offerings in the Bible began with Cain and Abel, the first generation born to man. Perhaps Adam or Eve started the practice, but there is no record of it. Nor is there any record of a law or command that required offerings. Cain and Abel simply did it.

Abel was a shepherd, so he gave to God a part of what he had. He gave sheep. His offering came from the best he had, and he gave it without delay. His actions spoke volumes about his thoughts and his purpose. God had blessed Abel with his flocks, and Abel was eager to show his gratitude by returning an offering to God.

God respected the offering, and more importantly, God respected Abel. God did not demand anything. He did not require Abel to give anything that he did not have, or to deliver any lambs before they were born. For his simple, humble act of gratitude, Abel received the respect of God.

As we continue on our pilgrim journey, are we genuinely grateful for God's blessings? Do we seek to honor God? What are we giving? If it is time, is it the first time that we schedule, and is it our best time? If it is money, do we give cheerfully or grudgingly? Are we eager to make our offering to God? Could God respect us or our offering the way that God respected Abel? In short, are we honoring God in God's way?

Generous heavenly Father, I am grateful for your blessings and amazed by your generosity. Every day you provide for me, and in my need you provide abundantly. Give me joy in my offerings to you. Make me eager to return a portion of your blessings so that you will know that my heart finds happiness in you, and not in the things that you have given me. In the name of Jesus, your Son and my Savior, Amen.

Honoring God in Our Way

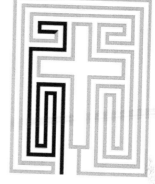

Cain brought of the fruit of the ground an offering unto the LORD. . . . But unto Cain and to his offering God had not respect. Genesis 4:3b, 5a

Cain brought an offering to God, but God didn't have respect for Cain or the offering. Yesterday we considered Abel and his offering. God had respect for them. What was the difference? The scripture doesn't say directly. We know that Abel gave from the first and best of his flock. There is no mention of this with Cain. Maybe Cain was taking his own share first. Maybe he was keeping the best part for himself. No one really knows. He was giving to God, but he was doing it in his own way and on his own terms.

A few thousand years later, Jesus was in Jerusalem. People brought money and offered it to God. There were some who gave lavish gifts, and there was a widow gave two copper coins. Jesus saw her and told the disciples that the woman had given more than the others. What was the difference? Jesus must have seen the confusion on his disciples' faces. He explained that the widow gave all she had; the other people had plenty, and only gave some of their left over money. The wealthier people honored God, but only on their own terms, and only after they had provided for themselves. The woman gave on God's terms. Although she remains nameless, she was honored by the Lord.

Today we go to church. We put cash into the offering plate. Are we like Abel or Cain? Are we like the widow or the rich people? Are we honoring God in God's way by placing Him first, or are we honoring God in our own way, simply giving Him a portion of our surplus after caring for ourselves?

On our pilgrimage, we are seeking to encounter God. We cannot do this unless we place Him first. We must honor Him in His way. If we only honor God on our own terms, we make Him second. That is not the way that we are called. That is not the path to follow. Put God first.

Gracious God and creator of all, your very name is holy and pure. You are alpha and omega, the first and the last. Show me your way, for your way is the only way. Let me walk in your path, see through your eyes, and hear through your ears. Let me honor you in all that I do. Let me honor you on your terms, Lord, let me honor you in your way. Amen.

Relationships Gone Awry

And the LORD said unto Cain, Why art thou wroth? and why is thy countenance fallen?
Genesis 4:6

When God showed no respect for Cain's offerings, Cain became angry. The King James Version says he was "wroth," which is wrathful or extremely angry. God saw the problem. He tried to counsel Cain. God told him what he needed to do. God told him that unless he got control of the situation, sin would pull him down.

The scripture doesn't say that Cain ever acknowledged or responded to God. He had already closed his mind and his heart to God's advice. Rather than hearing the words that could save him, Cain nurtured his rage, and then he turned it against his brother. He invited Abel to go out to the field. Once there, he committed the first murder ever recorded.

That murder was more than a physical act. It was the product of relationships that had gone bad. Cain had no relationship with God, or he could have heard and followed God's advice. Cain had a poor relationship with Abel, or Cain would not have directed his rage against his brother. Cain had no relationship with his parents, or he could have sought help or advice from Adam or Eve.

We must take a lesson about relationships from Cain's story. When God asked Cain about Abel, Cain retorted with the question, "Am I my brother's keeper?" In one sense, Cain had a point. He was not his brother's keeper, but he was still his brother's brother. He was not responsible for Adam or Eve, either, but he was still his parents' child. He was not accountable for God, but he was still accountable to God. Breaking one relationship was hard, but it led to a pattern of broken relationships, deep unhappiness, consuming rage, and murder.

On our pilgrimage we are seeking a deeper relationship with God. That cannot be achieved unless there is a relationship to build on. How is your relationship with God? With your family? With your neighbors?

With each path, with each step, think about your relationship with God. Think about your relationship with those around you. Pray about your relationships. Listen to God, and heed His counsel. We are not destined for Cain's mistakes. We are destined for God. We are destined for glory.

God of love, your voice in my heart is sweet. It calls me to a tender and loving relationship with you. It calls me to be tender and loving to those around me. Keep my ears always open to your voice, my mind always open to your counsel, and my heart always open to your love. In the name of your loving Son, Jesus, Amen.

Action and Reaction

And Cain said to the LORD, My punishment is greater than I can bear. Behold, you have driven me out this day from the face of the earth; and from your face shall I be hid; and I shall be a fugitive and a vagabond in the earth; and it shall come to pass, that every one that finds me shall slay me. Genesis 4:13-14

Consequences can be difficult to appreciate without personal experience. Unfortunately, personal experience is not available until after decisions are made and actions are taken. We can try our best to predict outcomes. We can prepare for different possibilities. But the true consequences for any action are rarely known in advance.

When Adam and Eve ate the forbidden fruit, they sinned against God. As a consequence, they were separated from God. Cain murdered his brother, Abel. This was different. It was an unprecedented action and it led to unprecedented consequences. By killing his brother, Cain sinned against God and he also sinned against man. As a consequence, Cain was separated from God and he was also outcast from all other people. He would be a nomad and a wanderer; he would be a person scorned by all.

Cain's reaction to the consequences for committing murder is instructive for us today. Rather than expressing any remorse or accepting responsibility for Abel's death, Cain complained that his punishment was too much to bear. Ironically, even though he had killed Abel without hesitation, Cain despaired because other people might kill him. In God's infinite wisdom and mercy He placed a mark on Cain to protect him, but there is no indication that Cain ever sought to reconcile himself with God or with other people. A short lineage of Cain appears in the fourth chapter of Genesis. His descendants were destroyed in the flood. His name never appears again in the Old Testament. In the New Testament he is seldom mentioned, and only negatively.

In contrast with Cain, a thief hanging on a cross acknowledged that he had done wrong and deserved punishment—even the punishment of death. He asked Jesus to remember him. To a repentant soul, Jesus promised paradise.

We are all human. On our pilgrimage to the foot of the cross we will make mistakes. How will we react to God's correction? Will we complain about our punishment, or will we repent from evil and seek God's glory? The choice is ours to make.

Holy, pure, and perfect God, I come to you knowing that I am a sinner. I sin against you, and I sin against people. I know that your judgment is just. I also know that your mercy is great. Lord, I do not want anything to separate us. I desire only to be with you and to share in fellowship with your children. I am sorry for the wrong I have done. By your grace, I will seek to walk only on your path so that one day I may know your paradise. Amen.

A Habit of Decay

And God saw that the wickedness of man was great in the earth, and that every imagination of the thoughts of his heart was only evil continually. Genesis 6:5

Every generation complains about the declining morals or ethics of the next generation. Adam and Eve ate the forbidden fruit. They fell under a curse of death, but they didn't hurt anyone else. It wasn't until Cain that anyone committed murder, and that was much worse, right?

Even though Cain was cast out, God established rules to keep others from harming him. Sadly, a few generations later, Cain's descendant Lamech converted God's rules into a threat of vengeance against others. In Lamech's heart, God's rule of mercy and protection had become a tool of terror and destruction.

The deterioration continued generation by generation until the days of Noah. By the time we reach chapter 6 of Genesis, the thoughts of men were only evil all of the time. But there was Noah. He was righteous in God's eyes. God told Noah to build an ark so that he and his family would be saved. Noah never questioned God's instruction. He humbly listened, and he humbly obeyed.

The scriptures describe the ark. It was a big undertaking. It would have taken many years to build. The entire community would have seen it. Word of Noah's project would have spread. During that time, though, there is not even one report of a person who was inspired to live a righteous life. The habits of violence and evil had become pervasive. Only Noah and his family were spared from the destruction of the great flood, and they survived only because they received God's mercy.

What habits do we have today? Do we have habits of righteousness or habits of evil? On a pilgrimage to encounter God, we cannot tolerate evil habits in ourselves. It does not matter that another generation has worse habits. It does not matter that our sense of ethics is better than someone else's. The habit of decay which has been a part of humanity since the beginning of the earth has no place on this journey. Our goal and our destination is communion with God. Only God's standards apply. We must aspire to righteousness before God, and we have to remember that this is achievable only through God's mercy and grace.

Holy God, I am not righteous. I am sinful. You are holy. You are pure. Show mercy to me, Lord. Show me your way, and give me the humility to submit to your will. Grant me your grace, that I may come to you and commune with you. This is my heart's greatest desire. Amen

In the Calm After the Storm

And God remembered Noah, and every living thing, and all the cattle that was with him in the ark: and God made a wind to pass over the earth, and the waters assuaged. Genesis 8:1

Modern translations of the scriptures are wonderful tools. They are written in contemporary language using words that are usually easier for us to understand. Replacing archaic language can make passages more approachable, especially for younger readers.

Sometimes, though, things get lost in the translation—or in the re-translation. The King James Version of Genesis 8:1 has language that is worth revisiting. In that version, the last phrase says that "the waters assuaged." Assuaged? What does that mean? It means to lessen the intensity of something that pains or distresses: to pacify, or quiet: to put to an end by satisfying. "Relieve" is a synonym. The verse has a wonderful meaning when read with that definition. After God made the winds blow, He made the waters give relief. The same waters that had caused so much destruction were used by God to pacify everyone in the ark, to quiet their spirits, to satisfy their souls. There was calm after the storm.

When winds blow against a large boat, water splashes against its hull, not destructively, but firmly. Like the passengers on the ark, boats today are designed to keep their passengers safe. The sound of waves against the hull is soothing. It is comforting. To say it another way, the waters assuage.

Modern translations which say that the water receded or subsided are accurate. There is nothing wrong with them. They still tell us that trials do not last forever, and God will bring an end to difficult times. While we are on our pilgrim journey, though, don't miss the other meanings. Don't forget that God's awesome power assuages. It can be a source of comfort to the righteous. In our walk day by day, there can be calm after the storm.

Almighty God, your awesome power scares me sometimes. It is too great for me to understand. Yet I know that you love me. You have provided safety for my soul. Give me peace in your power, comfort in your strength, and joy in your mighty arms. Remind me that you are caring for me in the storms of my life, and that you will send calm after every storm. Amen.

Peace in Promise

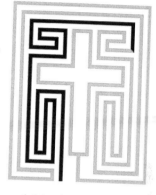

I do set my bow in the cloud, and it shall be for a token of a covenant between me and the earth.
Genesis 9:13

It is one thing to experience the calm after the storm. It is something else altogether to find peace. How long did it take Noah and his family to find peace? The ordeal on board the ark lasted much longer than most people realize. Scripture tells us that during the flood, rains fell on the earth for forty days and forty nights. Water flooded the earth for 150 days before the ark touched ground. Two or three months later the mountain tops could be seen. A couple of months after that, Noah celebrated the new year by taking the cover off of the ark. Finally, after nearly two more months, the ground was dry enough to leave the ark.

Noah and his family had entered the ark "on the seventeenth day of the second month." They left the ark on "the twenty-seventh day of the second month" the following year—just over a full year later. Everything had changed. Everyone was gone. The storm that flooded the earth was over, but where could Noah find peace? God provided the answer. God said, "Don't worry. This will never happen again. Here's my rainbow. When I see it, I will remember." When we see it, we can remember, too.

On this third Sunday during Lent, look to the skies. If the skies are blue, admire its beauty and thank God. If you see a rainbow, rejoice in God's promise. If you see only clouds, remember that this is where God has set His rainbows. The rains will stop. The clouds will part. The light will shine. God has made His covenant, and God is always faithful. From before the Christian era to the present, from eternity to eternity, God never fails. Hallelujah!

Holy God, you are the god of peace. You give peace after the storm. You give peace between people. You give peace to my soul. Thank you for your promises. They are precious to me. They give me comfort. They give me peace. Make me ever mindful of your promises which are revealed in creation all around me, and fill me with the calm assurance that you care for me day by day. In your Son's holy name I pray, Amen.

People of God's Choosing

This week focuses on people chosen by God to fill important roles in His plan for the world, and their responses to His calling.

Choosing Abram

Now the LORD had said unto Abram, Get yourself out of your country, and from your kindred, and from your father's house, unto a land that I will show you. Genesis 12:1

Some stories are amazing. Against all odds, unexpected events occur. Underdogs prevail. Unlikely heroes save the day. We are at a loss to explain why or how these things happen. They just do.

The book of Genesis provides a family tree leading up to the birth of Abram. Then it says that God called Abram to go to a new land. It doesn't tell us why. The Hebrew Midrash includes some stories about Abram that reveal how he came to recognize God and reject idols, but nothing explains God's decision. When we think about it, though, are we ever entitled to an explanation for God's choices? If we were bold enough to ask God for a justification, it is likely that we would receive the same answer that Job received when he questioned God. There is no way to summarize God's response. Just read Job chapters 38 through 41. The phrase, "Because I said so," really doesn't capture it.

Perhaps the writer of Genesis understood that we are not entitled to an explanation for God's choices. Maybe that is why there is no attempt to explain it. Even though we don't know why God chose Abram, we can still learn from it. We can learn that God makes His own choices for His own reasons. We can learn that God's choices lead to blessing. We can learn that answering God's call is the only thing that we really need to do.

On our pilgrim journey, listen for God. Answer His call.

God, I don't understand you. I know that in this life I can never really understand you. I was not there when you laid the foundations of the earth, but I know that you were there. I don't know how you created life, but I know that you did. I don't know why you love me. I only know that you do. Thank you for choosing Abram for his journey. Thank you for choosing me for this one. I know that you are on the path that I should follow. Let me be always open to your calling and obedient to your word. Amen.

Choosing Rebekah

Let the same be she that you have appointed for your servant Isaac.
Genesis 24:14c

People approach choices in different ways. Some people want to control the decision making process. They gather as much information as they can, organize it meticulously, and evaluate it systematically. Every detail is parsed and examined. A decision is made only after every issue and every option has been thoroughly considered. Other people are more inclined to "flip a coin" or leave decisions to someone else.

The story of Rebekah becoming Isaac's wife is filled with many choices and decisions. The most important one, though, is barely mentioned. Abraham decided that Isaac needed a wife, so he sent a servant to find her. The servant discussed Abraham's instructions at length with him and began the journey. After he found Rebekah, he met with her brother, father, and mother. They had a long discussion and made more decisions, and Rebekah decided when she would leave. Upon the servant's return, Isaac and Rebekah saw each other and their life together began.

Something important was left out of this summary. It is the part about the servant's prayer. This nameless servant did an amazing and wonderful thing. He did not ask God to help him choose a good wife for Isaac. Instead, he asked God to reveal the wife that God had already chosen. The servant recognized that God's choice was the only one that mattered.

God has wonderful plans for our lives. Along the way, we have to make choices and decisions. Like the servant sent by Abraham, though, our best choice will always be to follow God and listen to Him. When we walk with God, we can know His paths. When we listen to God, we can know His will. When we do God's will, we are blessed.

God in heaven, thank you for the wonderful plan you have for my life. You have placed your path before me. You have spoken your words to me. Let me know the joy of obedience to your will. Wherever you lead, I will follow. What you say, I will hear. What you teach, I will write upon my heart. When the path is easy, let me rejoice in your light. When the path becomes harsh or difficult, give me the courage and strength to follow you. Amen.

Choosing Israel

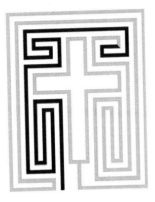

Thy name shall be called no more Jacob, but Israel. Genesis 32:28

Good things happen. Sometimes they happen in spite of us. That probably sounds like a strange statement, but consider it in this context. A woman conceived twin sons. The boys began fighting even before they were born. She asked God to explain what was happening. The Lord told her that her children would be contentious, and that the older child would serve the younger.

The twins were still fighting at birth. As the first arrived, the second was grabbing his heel. The older twin was named for his appearance. He was Esau, or "hairy." The younger twin was named for his conduct. He was Jacob, which means "heel grabber." Being a heel grabber wasn't just a silly name. It was a phrase for someone who tricks or deceives other people, much like "pulling your leg" today, but without a humorous side.

Over the years, the boys grew into their names. Esau became hairier; Jacob became trickier. Jacob's tricks eventually enraged Esau to the point that Jacob had to run for his life. Even as he ran, though, God gave Jacob a vision of blessing. For the next several years Jacob began amassing wealth while working for his uncle, Laban. He also learned about being on the receiving end of schemes and tricks when his uncle switched brides on him at his wedding.

Eventually Jacob began a journey to return home. Before the journey's end, he got into a fight with God. He struggled with God all night, and insisted on receiving God's blessing. At the end of the fight, God gave Jacob a new name. Instead of being the heel grabber, he became Israel, one who contends with God.

Jacob had plenty of experience for his new name. He had contended with Esau and Isaac. He had contended with Laban. Finally, he even contended with God. Through it all, God was shaping and molding him. God had chosen Israel to be a part of God's plan to bless the world. Being able to contend and overcome would be important for God's people, and it remains important today in the Christian era.

On our pilgrim journey we will encounter obstacles and difficulties. We may try to rely on our own craftiness for a while, but in the end we have to learn to face God and deal with His rules and demands. To fulfill God's calling in our lives, we have to set aside trickery and deceit and seek God's blessings.

God, thank you for your blessings. Thank you for giving me a hunger to be blessed. I am sorry for those times when I try to trick my way into receiving your blessings. Help me to remember that I will only realize your greatest blessings when I set aside all deceit and face you honestly. In Jesus' name I pray, Amen.

Choosing Moses

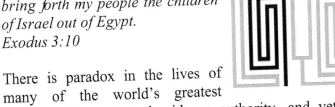

Come now therefore, and I will send you to Pharaoh, that you may bring forth my people the children of Israel out of Egypt.
Exodus 3:10

There is paradox in the lives of many of the world's greatest leaders. Some started with no authority, and yet they became very powerful leaders. Some were raised with the mantle of leadership, but they became powerless over time. So it was with Moses, a slave among leaders, and a leader among slaves.

Born the son of slaves, Moses' mother set him afloat on the Nile in hopes that his little raft would carry him to safety. Not only did God carry him to safety, but he became the son of royalty. He was literally a slave among leaders.

As he grew, he discovered his humble origins. One day, enraged at the treatment of his people, he killed an Egyptian. Instead of winning the admiration of the slaves, though, he found himself scorned by them. He was a leader among slaves, but he was not one of them. He found no acceptance and no home among them.

Moses fled from Egypt to escape the Pharaoh's anger, leaving behind all of his prior status and privilege. Although he had been raised with the mantle of leadership in Egypt, he had become powerless.

Many years later, Moses came face to face—or face to flame—with God. It was there that God called him to lead. Moses was not called to lead Egypt in the way that he had been raised by men. Instead, Moses was called to lead slaves in the way that he had been prepared by God. It had been a long process. God chose Moses as an infant, preparing him with education and training that he never would have received as a slave. God chose Moses as an exile when he was on the run from Pharaoh, preparing him with wilderness experience that he never would have gained inside of Pharaoh's palace walls. God chose Moses, and He sent Moses to fill the role that he was so uniquely prepared to fill.

God chooses us, too. Before He sends us, though, He prepares us, just as He prepared Moses. It would have made sense in human terms for Moses to assume the throne over Egypt and use that power to release God's people, but that is not what God chose to do. God chose to show the paradox of power. The humble were lifted up and the mighty were laid low. If we want to be used by God, we must also humble ourselves.

Heavenly Father, choose me. Choose me to lead, or choose me to serve. Prepare me with the knowledge and experience that I need so that I can faithfully answer your calling for my life. Whether you place me in the palace or in the wilderness, give me a grateful heart that rejoices in your blessings. Lay low my pride and arrogance, and teach me to serve with humility so that you alone will be glorified. Amen.

Choosing Joshua

And the LORD said to Moses, Take Joshua the son of Nun, a man in whom is the spirit, and lay your hand upon him. Numbers 27:18

Some people answer God's call so consistently that every step simply blends into the rest of God's plan. Their walk with God is so natural that even when they play a central role, glory goes to God alone. Joshua was that kind of person.

Joshua was actively involved in the history of the Israelites for roughly a century. As a youth he was Moses' aide. As a young man he was among the twelve spies sent by Moses to explore the land of Canaan. He was one of the two who urged the Israelites to have faith in God and enter the land.

When Moses grew old, God chose Joshua to assume the mantle of leadership. This new role was a natural continuation for Joshua. He was Israel's leader when God toppled the walls of Jericho in a miraculous and decisive battle. In the following years Joshua would lead the people to possess the promised land. Before he died at the age of one hundred ten, Joshua challenged the people to choose who they would serve. That was when he made his famous proclamation, "As for me and my house, we will serve the LORD."

Joshua faced many challenges and obstacles as the leader of Israel, but he did not face the kind of inner struggle that seemed to plague many other leaders. Joshua never hid

50

from God, and he never had to. At the end of his life when he challenged the Israelites to choose God, it was not because of a new revelation or a change in his understanding of God. Choosing God had been his only way of life for over a century.

There are obvious reasons to choose God while we are focused on our pilgrim journey. Our challenge, though, is to live like Joshua all of the time. Our challenge is to choose God with every breath we breathe, with every thought we think, with every act we do. Joshua's challenge to the Israelites is still a challenge to us today. Choose God.

Eternal God, thank you for the example of your servant Joshua. Joshua lived a long life—more than one hundred years. As long as that was, though, in your eternal reign, Joshua's life lasted only a brief moment. Even so, Lord, from before the Christian era through the end of all time, Joshua's life has eternal significance because every day he made an eternal choice. Every day, Lord, Joshua chose you. Give me the wisdom and the courage to do likewise. Lord, today I choose you. Amen.

Choosing David

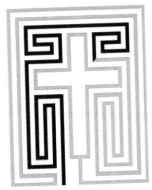

Then Samuel took the horn of oil, and anointed David in the midst of his brethren: and the Spirit of the LORD came upon David from that day forward. 1 Samuel 16:13a

Samuel was a great prophet, the last of the judges. He learned to recognize God's voice at an early age. Using that gift, Samuel listened to God's direction and anointed Saul as king over Israel. Not long afterward, God told Samuel to anoint someone else to be king.

Stop for a moment to think about this. Royal families do not like to be replaced. This was not likely to be a smooth transition. From Saul's perspective, it would be treason for Samuel to anoint someone else to take the throne, and treason was a capital offense. The danger was obvious to Samuel. Answering God's call to anoint a successor literally put Samuel's life in peril. Even so, he followed God's direction. He found David and anointed him.

Having anointed David, Samuel's life was no longer the only one at risk. A charge of treason would apply equally to David, and to prevent any of David's family members from claiming the throne, Saul might have killed them, too. Thus, through an act of obedience and blessing, Samuel, David, and David's family all found themselves in harm's way.

In the following years, David would rise in popularity, only to be declared an enemy of the state. He would lead a civil insurrection, and eventually take the throne. It was not a safe path. It was not an easy life. But it was the path that God had laid. It was the life that God had given. It was the way to blessing and fulfillment. It was the way to glorify God.

Being chosen by God does not mean that we will never face peril. While we honor God's calling, though, it does mean that we have God's care and blessing. As we continue on our pilgrimage, remember that God may call us to serve in dangerous places. The path He puts before us may lead through valleys and shadows. But God will still be with us. God will always care for us. He is our God, and we are His people.

Loving Father, thank you for watching over your children. Thank you for watching over me. Let me listen to your voice, just as Samuel did. Let me heed your call. Let me follow your path. Let me face danger for you, and let me know your blessings and your care. I know that when you care for me, there is nothing else that I need. Amen.

Peace in Promise

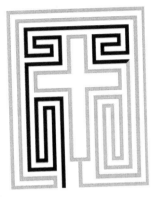

My covenant is with you.
Genesis 17:4

Along our pilgrim journey we have seen that God calls people to do things they would never do on their own. Noah built an ark in an age when there had been no rain. Abram left his homeland for a place he had never seen. Rebekah left her family to marry a man she had never met. Israel stopped using tricks to get ahead and began facing his challenges with God and with man. Moses left his palaces, and then he left his flocks. Joshua the aide became Joshua the commander. David the shepherd became David the king.

David would have accomplished nothing by building an ark. That was God's command to Noah many centuries earlier. Abram would have achieved nothing by marching around the city of Jericho. That would be God's command to Joshua a few centuries later. All of these people lived in different times and under different circumstances. They had different callings. They had different missions.

They had similarities, too. Each one listened to God's voice. Each one obeyed God's voice. Each one enjoyed God's blessing through obedience. In the face of danger and uncertainty, each one experienced peace in the promise of God.

We live in different times, and under circumstances different from those of the men and women in the Bible.

We have different callings and different missions. But we can each listen to God. We can choose to obey. We can enjoy God's blessings through obedience. We can experience peace in the promises of God.

Take time to rest in God's peace on this Lord's day. Listen. Obey. Enjoy. God's promises are for you.

God of peace, I praise you for your promises. Thank you for the promises that you made to the men and women of the Bible. Thank you for the witness of your faithfulness that we find in the scriptures. Thank you for your promises to me. I know that you are able to keep your promises, and I know that you are faithful to keep them. Let my life reflect my gratitude to you, and give me peace in the knowledge of your faithfulness. Amen.

Division and Demise

God gave His law to guide us while we waited for God's perfect salvation. As in the Garden of Eden, we could not follow God's rules. This week considers the division and downfall that we face when we break God's rules and rely on our own strength.

A Family Divided

And Absalom spoke to his brother Amnon neither good nor bad: for Absalom hated Amnon, because he had forced his sister Tamar.
2 Samuel 13:22

David is called a man after God's own heart. Continually throughout the scriptures, both God and man comment on the heart of David and his devotion to God. Even so, David was human. He was fallible, and sometimes he failed. We have already considered his tragic choices with Bathsheba and Uriah. Everyone understands that David did terrible things in those stories. In fact, when Nathan confronted him with his sin, David was outraged by his own conduct. As much as David might have learned through his own sins, he failed to teach those lessons to his children.

Amnon was David's firstborn son and the heir apparent to the throne. Absalom was Amnon's half-brother. Amnon eyed his sister Tamar, a beautiful woman by all accounts. Admiring her loveliness was not enough, though. Amnon desired Tamar for himself, so he arranged for an intimate meeting with her. When Tamar did not return Amnon's affections, Amnon raped her. Absalom hated Amnon for what he had done to Tamar, and nursed that hatred for years until he made careful arrangements to kill him. Lust, rape, and murder had invaded the palace once again.

We know that David regretted his sins and suffered because of them. Surely he would not have wanted his sons to experience the pain that goes with that kind of deep, overwhelming guilt. Yet we never read that David was aware of what his sons were doing. We do not find where he counseled them to be Godly men. Instead we see the scheming members of a powerful family who were bent upon satisfying their sinful desires and thirst for vengeance. The family fell into a pattern of decay. The family was divided.

In our daily walk, what do people see in us? Do they see people after God's own heart, or do they see eyes filled with lust and vengeance? In our homes, do we show kindness and charity to our family, or do we demand our own way and carry grudges?

As we continue on our journey through the labyrinth to experience God more deeply, we have to remember that we are part of God's family. We must show love to our brothers and sisters. Where there is division, we must seek reunion; where there is hurt, healing; where there is despair, hope; where there is sadness, joy. There is only one path in the labyrinth. It is not divided. We must not be divided, either.

Holy Father, loving God, thank you for calling me to be your child. Create in me a clean heart—a heart like your own. Remind me that I am one of your children, and keep me ever mindful that you love all of your children, just as you love me. And as I am reminded of your love for my brothers and sisters, use me to show your love to them today and every day. In the name of Jesus, your Son who I love, Amen.

A Nation Divided

Thus says the LORD, the God of Israel, Behold, I will rend the kingdom out of the hand of Solomon, and will give ten tribes to thee. 1 Kings 11: 31

Solomon has been famous for his wisdom for nearly three thousand years. He was tested and challenged by people and rulers from the Euphrates and the lands of the Philistines to the border of Egypt, and he always provided wise answers. In spite of his great wisdom, though, Solomon allowed foolishness to invade his kingdom. Even as he constructed a beautiful temple to worship the one true God in Jerusalem, he allowed the worship of false gods throughout the land. As a consequence, God divided the kingdom following Solomon's death. Rehoboam, Solomon's son, remained king in Jerusalem with two tribes, Benjamin and Judah. The other ten tribes separated themselves and followed Jeroboam.

Solomon never tried to divide Israel; he tried to increase its wealth and influence. In the process, though, he lost his focus. He could have made a conscious choice day by day to place God first in every decision. He could have used his life and his position to inspire and influence others to worship the Creator of the world. Instead, in order to achieve wealth and influence, he recognized the worship of false gods. He accepted religious division. He elevated worldly goals above heavenly ideals.

In a very real sense, the division of Israel occurred long before Solomon's death. It occurred when Solomon chose to place worldly riches and influence ahead of his commitment to honor God. Through the eyes of men, Solomon's kingdom was united and great. Through the eyes of God, it was divided and broken.

Solomon observed that there is nothing new under the sun. He was right. On our journey to encounter God, we have to face the same choices that Solomon did. Will we commit our lives to honor God first, or will we focus on something else? Will we choose to glorify God, or will we seek glory for ourselves, our country, or our cause? If we place God first, everything else will fall into place. If we place God second, everything else will fall apart. Make the conscious choice today to glorify God.

Mighty God, you have made this world, and you are the one Creator over all of it. I acknowledge you as the one, true God. May all the world recognize you as I do. Give me strength and courage to see the world as you see it, and to live in unity with my neighbors. Make me a healer of nations, not by accepting false idols, but by spreading the Gospel of your Son and living my life as a beacon of your love. Amen.

Protection

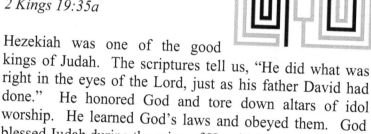

And it came to pass that night, that the angel of the LORD went out, and smote in the camp of the Assyrians an hundred fourscore and five thousand.
2 Kings 19:35a

Hezekiah was one of the good kings of Judah. The scriptures tell us, "He did what was right in the eyes of the Lord, just as his father David had done." He honored God and tore down altars of idol worship. He learned God's laws and obeyed them. God blessed Judah during the reign of Hezekiah.

The Assyrian empire was one of the great world powers in the days of King Hezekiah. It had conquered the northern tribes of Israel and captured many cities in the southern kingdom of Judah as well. Sennacherib, the king of Assyria, sent one of his commanders to jeer at the people in Jerusalem. The commander stood outside the city walls and shouted at the top of his lungs. He proclaimed the might of his king. He expressed contempt for Judah's allies. He belittled Hezekiah and denied the power of God.

Hezekiah must have considered his options. He had tried to buy peace from Sennacherib once before. Gold had been stripped from the temple doors and given as tribute. Hezekiah had nothing better to offer, and the armies of the Assyrian king had come back again to wage war. Hezekiah also knew that fighting was out of the question. Any way that you looked at the military situation, Jerusalem did not have a chance in the world. Even so, Hezekiah did not give in to defeat. He did not need a chance in the world because he knew that his hope was in the Lord. In an impassioned prayer he asked God, "Now, O Lord our God, deliver us from his hand, so that all kingdoms on earth may know that you alone, O Lord, are God." God's angel devastated the enemy. One hundred eighty-five thousand solders were slain. The invading army withdrew. Jerusalem was saved.

The world may seem overpowering to us today, too. We may be penniless and feel powerless over the circumstances facing us. As we walk with God, though, we can learn from Hezekiah's faith and God's faithfulness. God loves His people, and He protects His faithful servants.

Mighty God, you are my God. No one and nothing can withstand your glory and your power. I submit my life humbly to serve you, giving you all of the honor and the glory and the praise. Let me hunger to know your laws and to obey them. Now protect me, and keep all of your people safe from harm. Because of your care and loving kindness, let all kingdoms on earth know that you alone, O Lord, are God. Amen.

Peril

Your eyes shall not see all the evil which I will bring upon this place.
2 Kings 22:20b

Recent reports of artifacts found in the Holy Land reflect a society that worshiped many different gods before the time of Christ. Some skeptics urge that these relics undermine the Old Testament scriptures. On the contrary, they are sadly consistent with the stories recorded in the books of Kings and Chronicles. Many kings of Israel and Judah failed to honor God. They set up monuments and altars to false gods. They dedicated horses and chariots to idols in Solomon's temple. They offered sacrifices—even human sacrifices—to the pagan deities of surrounding communities.

Among the kings of Judah, Manasseh was especially evil. His name sounds like the Hebrew word "forget." It was the name that Joseph, the son of Israel, gave to his first son in Egypt. Joseph chose the name because he was forgetting the pain that he suffered after being sold into slavery by his brothers. Ironically, King Manasseh was forgetting something, too. He was forgetting about Joseph. He was forgetting about the exodus from Egypt and the conquest of the Holy Land. He was forgetting about the success of David's kingdom and the blessings of Hezekiah. In a word, he was forgetting about God. King Manasseh worshiped false gods, offered his own son as a human sacrifice, and spilled the blood of innocents throughout Jerusalem. Things grew so bad that God finally decided to let Jerusalem experience disaster.

Manasseh died before Jerusalem fell. His son Amon reigned for two years before being assassinated. At that time, an eight-year-old boy named Josiah took the throne. Despite the peril looming over Jerusalem, Josiah honored God. He restored the temple and destroyed pagan altars throughout the kingdom. Celebration of the Passover, which had not been observed for decades, resumed in Jerusalem. The laws of Moses were once again taught and applied. Josiah could not change things that happened before his time. He could only choose his own path one step at a time. He chose well. Because Josiah was humble and obedient, God withheld judgment during his lifetime.

We cannot change past events, either. Whether we like it or not, some of those events have consequences and perils that loom over our lives. Like Josiah, though, we have the ability to choose our path one step at a time. We have already made the choice to follow a pilgrim journey to the foot of the cross. Don't fear the perils. Celebrate the joy of humble obedience.

Holy, holy, holy Lord, I bow myself before your awesome greatness. Your laws and your judgments are perfect. I am not worthy to come before you, and yet you welcome me with blessings and love. Thank you for your mercies and kindness toward me. Keep me safe from peril and lead me safely into your arms. In the name of Christ my Savior, Amen.

Destruction

For through the anger of the LORD it came to pass in Jerusalem and Judah, until he had cast them out from his presence.
2 Kings 24:20

Jonah is a famous prophet from Israel because he is the main character in one of the biggest fish stories ever recorded, but the fish is not a focus for this devotion. Instead, let's think about relationships, actions, and outcomes. The people in a city called Nineveh had no relationship with God. They were sinning and God was ready to put an end to it. First, though, he sent his prophet Jonah to warn them. When Jonah told Nineveh that God was angry and they were facing destruction, they repented. They sought a right relationship with God. The outcome was grace. God spared them.

The story of Israel is different. Its people had a covenant relationship with God from the time of Abraham. Through the power of God, Moses freed them from bondage in Egypt. They received God's law in the wilderness. Joshua led them back into the promised land. King David expanded the kingdom. God sent many prophets to guide them in the paths of righteousness. Israel was truly blessed by God. Unlike Nineveh, though, Israel turned away from God. Israel worshiped idols not once, but generation after generation. They broke their covenant. Their relationship with God deteriorated. The outcome was destruction. God cast Israel from His presence.

God still speaks today. He speaks through the scriptures and through His servants. We can open our ears and our hearts like the people of Nineveh, or we can close them. We can develop and nurture a relationship with God, or we can reject our Creator and Redeemer. The outcome is clear, and the outcome is eternal.

On our pilgrim journey to the foot of the cross, don't choose destruction. Listen to God. Seek a deeper relationship with Him. Act in humble obedience to His Word. Enjoy an outcome of blessing. Receive the joy of life.

Great God in heaven, I praise you for your mercy. Thank you for being such a gracious and compassionate God, slow to anger and abounding in steadfast love, a God who relents from sending destruction if I will only listen to your righteous words and seek to serve your perfect will. Let me always yearn for a deeper relationship with you. Let me live to serve you, and let me dwell in your house forever. Amen.

Prophecy

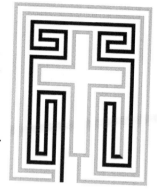

For unto us a child is born, unto us a son is given: and the government shall be upon his shoulder: and his name shall be called Wonderful, Counsellor, The mighty God, The everlasting Father, The Prince of Peace. Isaiah 9:6

So far, these pilgrim devotions have focused on the history of the Old Testament. That history is almost complete. We began with creation and the flood. We considered the people chosen by God and their leaders. We learned about kings and kingdoms. When we take the scripture lessons to heart, we are inspired by the successes and sharpened by the challenges that people have faced for thousands of years. We also take stock in the somber realities of failure, learning that in the end, God cast the nation of Judah from His presence. Even so, the end of one story often foreshadows the beginning of another, connecting the stories in a way that gives hope. Today's verse provides that kind of link between the Old Testament and New Testament scriptures.

After many centuries of moral decay, idol worship, and defeat, God sent a prophet to proclaim a message of great hope to a nation in exile. A child is born. He will be a leader. He will be wonderful, wise, and powerful. God Himself will come, His reign will last forever, and there will be real, lasting peace. Could there be a better message for a people who had been cast from the presence of God? A few more centuries would pass before Jesus, the Christ, would walk on the face of the earth, but this message of hope bridged that gap. In contrast with man-made idols, temples, and religions that have long since been forgotten, the hope that springs from this prophecy filled the hearts and minds of God's people, carrying forward a knowledge and a faith that still inspires us today.

Scholars today debate who Isaiah was or how many different people he might have been. They argue whether the book of Isaiah should be split into multiple books. They wrangle with translation of the Hebrew text and the phrasing of the words. In the midst of all of the intellectual bickering, though, there is a truth. God is God, and God gives hope. The hope of a new child. The hope of a new day. The hope of a new peace. Hope.

Most of our journey to the foot of the cross is behind us. Many steps and many stories are complete. Yet, we have not reached our destination. We still seek the cross. We still seek God. As we continue the journey, remember that, like the people of Isaiah's time, it is hope that carries us forward, and it is God who gives us hope.

Everlasting Father, you were here in the beginning. You will be here in the end. And you are here with me now. I marvel at your eternal nature. You are too wonderful and too great for me to understand. Thank you for walking with me. Thank you for giving me hope. I love you. Truly, I love you. Amen.

Peace in Promise

If my people, which are called by my name, shall humble themselves, and pray, and seek my face, and turn from their wicked ways; then will I hear from heaven, and will forgive their sin, and will heal their land. 2 Chronicles 7:14

King David's family experienced division. The nation of Israel split into separate kingdoms. Invaders swept across the land. In the end, the nation of Israel was conquered. The temple was destroyed. The people were exiled. They had no home. There was no peace.

These tragedies were not the whole story, though. King David conquered many lands. Solomon was famous for his wisdom. God saved Jerusalem from Sennacherib's armies. There were good kings and times of great blessing. Israel had a home land and times of peace.

What distinguishes these stories? Why were there times of blessing and times of sorrow? Why did Israel experience success and failure? Is there an answer?

Edmund Burke, a statesman and philosopher of the 18th century, is quoted as saying, "Those who don't know history are destined to repeat it." This may be true, but it can also be said that those who do know history can enjoy the blessing of repeating it. Through God's divine inspiration, the Chronicler recorded one of the very precious promises in the Old Testament. "If my people, which are called by my name, shall humble themselves, and pray, and seek my face, and turn from their wicked ways; then will I hear from heaven, and will forgive their sin, and will heal their land." When Israel followed God's words, they experienced blessing. We know this. The process is really quite simple. Pray, obey, and repeat. Do we have the courage to repeat history?

God has come, as He promised. Christ walked among us, and today Christians are people who are called by His name. On this day, the fifth Sunday during Lent, let us humble ourselves, and pray, and seek God's face, and turn from our wicked ways. God will hear. God will forgive. God will heal us.

God of every blessing, I praise your holy name. Thank you for your boundless grace, through which I can be called by your name. I hunger for your blessings, both for me and for my neighbor, the nation, and your world. I know that you bless the humble. Lord God, give me a humble heart. Let me seek your face. Let me repent from every sin and from every wicked thought and deed. I know, Lord, that you are faithful. Thank you for hearing me. Grant me your forgiveness. Heal me, Lord. Heal and bless this land. Amen.

The Savior Comes

Our survey of Old Testament stories is finished. Devotions this week focus on the coming of Christ and His preparation for ministry.

Something to Ponder

But Mary kept all these things, and pondered them in her heart.
Luke 2:19

As a young woman, Mary had some truly extraordinary experiences. An angel visited her with news that she would bear God's son. She conceived a child even though she was a virgin. Her fiancé, Joseph, considered calling off their wedding, but an angel visited him, too, and told him to wed Mary and raise the child. Mary visited her cousin, Elizabeth, who, by inspiration from the Holy Spirit, acknowledged the Lordship of Mary's son. Elizabeth was expecting a child, too, just as her husband, Zechariah, had been told by an angel.

That year Rome declared a census, so Joseph and Mary had to journey across the countryside just as her due date arrived. At their destination in Bethlehem they had nowhere to stay, and they had to settle for a stable. There her son Jesus was born.

Shepherds came to worship the child in the stable and shared the news that they, too, had been visited by angels. In his gospel account, Luke tells us that after the shepherds' visit, Mary treasured these things and pondered them in her heart.

Little did Mary know, but the events of that unusual year were only the beginning. She had no way of knowing what the coming decades held in store for her: how her son would inspire crowds of people with his teaching and miracles; how the priests and leaders would plot and scheme to destroy him; how he would be beaten, abused, and crucified; how he would rise from the grave and ascend into heaven.

Mary lived through all of this. She faced the glory of angels, witnessed unexplainable miracles, experienced unspeakable grief, and rejoiced in the victory of life. Yet, it was after the most ordinary thing—the visit of the shepherds—that the scriptures tell us she stopped to ponder. God's presence was with her throughout her extraordinary experiences, and God was with her in the ordinary events, too.

On our journey to the foot of the cross we will encounter and experience the extraordinary presence of God. We will feel God's love and know His grace. As we go, though, we need to remember that God is always at work in the ordinary world around us. Just as God was present in the ordinary visit of ordinary shepherds, He is with us in our ordinary, everyday lives, too. That is something to ponder.

Holy God, may your name be glorified in all the earth. Give to me vision to see your work and words to proclaim your greatness. Let me praise you in the extraordinary and spectacular things that you do, and also in the familiar, ordinary events of life. Give me pause to ponder your love, and a heart to share your love with all those around me. In your Son's glorious name, Amen.

Good Tidings of Great Joy

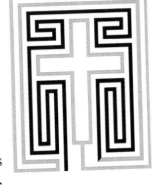

And the angel said unto them, Fear not: for, behold, I bring you good tidings of great joy, which shall be to all people. Luke 2:10

The story of the shepherds is featured in Christmas pageants, plays, and sermons every year, and it should be. What a tale it is! These simple, hard-working people received a personal invitation to celebrate the most wonderful birth in history. It was delivered by the heavenly host complete with fanfare and song. Imagine how special you would feel. In contrast, kings and rulers were unaware of what was happening. They were not even on the guest list.

The angels' greeting was much, much more than an invitation to the shepherds, though. That special invitation was given *to* the shepherds alone, but it was not given *for* them alone. The last words of Luke 2:10 are "all people." The shepherds received the invitation, but the joy was for the whole world. The good news—the very gospel of Jesus Christ—is for everyone. It is not just for shepherds and carpenters. It is not reserved for the rich and famous. It is for you. It is for me. It is for our neighbors. It is for the entire world. No wonder the shepherds were praising God at the end of the story. They returned to their ordinary routines, but they were filled with joy. It brings a smile to think about them returning along the roads outside Bethlehem, following the paths through the fields, and rehearsing this wonderful story to their flocks before sharing it with their families and friends.

74

On this pilgrimage, we are like the shepherds in a sense. We are on a pilgrim journey because, like the shepherds, we heard about it. Like the shepherds, we followed. Like the shepherds, we have found ourselves involved in something exciting and special. It is filled with lessons and experiences that we will carry for the rest of our lives. As special as this journey may be to us, though, God's path is not for us alone. God's path is for everyone. The cross is for everyone. Salvation is for everyone.

As you think about your journey today, consider the people you see who may not have heard the good news. Will they know about the joy you have in Christ? Will they see God's love in your life? Will they hear God's love in your words? Will they feel God's love in their hearts? You have good news of great joy. Share it!

Holy God who sent angels and called shepherds on that first Christmas night, thank you for calling me to follow this path. Thank you for revealing yourself to the shepherds in their time, and thank you for showing yourself to me today. Fill me with the joy that the shepherds knew. Fill me so that the joy of your presence shines in my life and in my words. Make me an instrument to share your love in the world today. In the name of your son, the Holy One of Israel, Amen.

Safe Journey

Take the young child and his mother, and flee into Egypt, and stay there until I bring you word. Matthew 2:13b

King Herod was disturbed when he learned that Magi had come to worship a child who was born to be king. Having fathered at least fifteen children, Herod was already in a quandary trying to designate his successor. To make things worse, the Magi had not come to honor any of Herod's children. They sought Jesus. Herod would not tolerate any threat to his authority or his legacy, so he did what any self-absorbed, power-mongering, would-be-despot would do. He ordered the execution of any child who might have been born since the time when the Magi saw a star in the sky.

God is so good. God is so faithful. He warned Joseph to take Jesus and Mary and go to Egypt. The account in the scriptures is brief, but it is rich with meaning. One lesson that we can take from this story is how much God is willing to give up because of His love for us. God, the Almighty Creator of heaven and earth, had no reason to fear Herod. Yet God, in the incarnate child Jesus, had made Himself vulnerable. He had become truly human, and this holy infant needed to escape from the wrath of an earthly king. He journeyed safely and stayed in Egypt until Herod died.

Like the infant Jesus, we are human. As humans, we are vulnerable. We are vulnerable to threats, and we are vulnerable to temptations. But praise be to God, whose loving care is over all creation, we can have joy in the face of threats. We can conquer every temptation. We can know fulfillment in every circumstance when we walk with God, because God will accomplish His perfect will for our lives.

Jesus' life was spared from Herod's wrath so that He could offer it in the fullness of time and save the world. Our journeys are different from the path that Jesus followed, but our mission is the same. We are here to offer our lives in service to God. God will give us the guidance and the warnings and the protection that we need to accomplish His plan for our lives. We are vulnerable, but God is good.

As you walk on your pilgrim journey today, praise God for His mercies. Thank Him for His loving kindness. Know that He will watch over you so that you can accomplish His perfect will for your life.

Great and wonderful God, creator of all and giver of life, thank you for coming as the Christ child. Thank you for your protection and your mercy. Thank you most of all for your boundless love. Just as Christ traveled safely, give me safe journey on your path. Guard over my life so that I may serve you. Amen.

Safe Return

Arise, and take the young child and his mother, and go into the land of Israel. Matthew 2:20

Returning is a frequent theme in the world around us. Ocean tides roll out only to return in their ordinary rhythm. Night falls in the evening, but day returns with the morning light. Animals follow regular patterns, too. Migratory birds soar across the skies, and then return to their origins year after year. Fish return to rivers where they spawn. The examples go on and on. There is something comforting in these regular, recurring events. They foster a sense of hope and security.

Returning is a frequent theme in the Bible, too. Jacob returned to the house of his father Isaac. The children of Israel returned from bondage to live in the promised land. Hebrew exiles in Babylon returned to rebuild Jerusalem. Jesus Christ returned safely to the land of Israel after His escape to Egypt. Just as the return of light and life in nature provides comfort in that setting, these stories of faith provide hope and assurance to our souls. Anger between brothers subsides. Oppression ends. Restoration really happens. And best of all, even in the form of a fragile infant, God is eternal and supreme. He outlasts and overcomes all.

The message of returning is important to us on our pilgrim journey, too. We will return from this pilgrimage to our daily lives, our homes, and our jobs, but we need to understand that our present path is a return journey of another kind. You see, we are alive because God breathed life into us. That is where we really began. We are seeking to encounter God, and we are returning to Him even now. The sense of comfort and security that we seek is at the end of this journey. The hope of spiritual fulfillment resides in God. Our destination is sure, and we desire a safe return— a return to God.

Eternal God, who was and is and is to come, your name is truly great. Creation is a reflection of your power and your love. Its regular order is a testament to your faithfulness and a comfort to my soul. I praise you for the inspiration of scripture, which gives me hope. Thank you for the life you have given me. Thank you for giving me a hunger for you. Grant me a safe return, oh God. Grant me a safe return to you. Amen.

Growing in Grace

And the child grew, and waxed strong in spirit, filled with wisdom: and the grace of God was upon him. Luke 2:40

Five hundred years before the Christian era, Heraclitus, a Greek philosopher, said that nothing endures but change. On its face the statement is appealing. In the biblical context, the story of creation is an account of change. The prophesies of the apocalypse foretell great and fearsome changes, too. In between we read of peace and war, love and hate. We learn of temples that were built and torn down, and kingdoms that rose and fell. Leaders came and went. All of them walked the earth, but only for a time. Abraham lived only once. Moses led only once. David reigned only once. All of them—*all of them*—are gone. Change followed change, and more change followed again.

As smart as he was, though, Heraclitus missed something very important. Indeed, he missed something that is central to our very existence. Change continues, but God endures. The scriptures tell of God enduring from before creation to the new Jerusalem and beyond. We read of God acting throughout history. We see God in the gift of life to every newborn child. We experience God's enduring love. We are saved by God's enduring grace. Yes, Heraclitus, change continues, but God endures.

The Gospels tell us that Jesus grew up in Nazareth. He experienced all of the changes that are common to all people. He grew in stature and strength and knowledge. He had a strong spirit and great wisdom. All the while, though, the enduring grace of the eternal God was upon him. The child Jesus changed and became a man, but God's grace never changed. It remained with Jesus, and it remains with us.

The grace of God was upon Jesus. The grace of God can be upon us as we continue our pilgrim journey, too. Pray for God's grace. Live in grace. Walk in grace. Grow in grace.

Gracious heavenly Father, I come into your eternal presence knowing that I am unworthy. I know that you are holy, and I know that I am sinful. I am in need of your salvation, and I stand in awe of your grace. Let me know your love, which lasts from eternity to eternity. Help me change, Lord, so that I can endure in your love and grow in your grace. Amen.

Celebration of Love

And the third day there was a marriage in Cana of Galilee; and the mother of Jesus was there: and both Jesus was called, and his disciples, to the marriage.
John 2:1-2

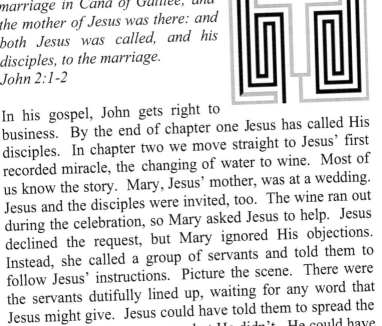

In his gospel, John gets right to business. By the end of chapter one Jesus has called His disciples. In chapter two we move straight to Jesus' first recorded miracle, the changing of water to wine. Most of us know the story. Mary, Jesus' mother, was at a wedding. Jesus and the disciples were invited, too. The wine ran out during the celebration, so Mary asked Jesus to help. Jesus declined the request, but Mary ignored His objections. Instead, she called a group of servants and told them to follow Jesus' instructions. Picture the scene. There were the servants dutifully lined up, waiting for any word that Jesus might give. Jesus could have told them to spread the word that the wine was gone, but He didn't. He could have told them to go buy more wine at the market, but He didn't. Instead, Jesus blessed a celebration of love right where He was, at the wedding in Cana. He had the servants fill jars with water, draw some out, and deliver it to the master of the banquet. The water became wine—very good wine— and the celebration continued.

The wedding celebration of love is a theme and a symbol throughout the Bible. God introduced marriage early in the scriptures at Genesis 2, where Adam and Eve are recognized as man and wife. The wedding in Cana took place early during the Jesus' earthly ministry, and Christ used marriage frequently to explain His teachings.

The importance of marriage as a celebration of love was not lost on John. In the last chapter of the last book of the Bible, John tells us, "The Spirit and the bride say, 'Come!' And let him who hears say, 'Come!' Whoever is thirsty, let him come; and whoever wishes, let him take the free gift of the water of life." Did you catch it? There is a bride. This is a wedding. It is a celebration of love. And they have miraculous water again. But this time it doesn't change to wine. This time, it is the water of life.

On your pilgrim journey, celebrate love right where you are. Celebrate love at weddings. Celebrate love in your home. Celebrate love in your work. Anywhere you are, celebrate love. God began the celebration long ago, and God will lead the celebration for eternity.

God of love, thank you for loving me. Thank you for the gift of love between man and wife. Thank you for the gift of love between mother and child. Thank you for the gift of love between friends. Thank you, Lord, for love. Let me celebrate your love, and let my life be a celebration of your love for all people. Amen.

Peace in Promise

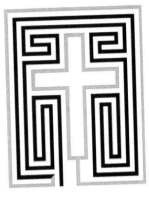

And she shall bring forth a son, and thou shalt call his name Jesus: for he shall save his people from their sins. Matthew 1:21

Our journey this week has followed Jesus' life up to the beginning of His ministry. From the miracle of Mary's conception to the changing of water to wine, there was no reason to question Jesus' divinity or His mission. Everything about Him had been a fulfillment of prophecy. If any doubt remained, the miracle at the wedding in Cana should have been enough to settle the issue once and for all. But it didn't. Instead, Jesus would face more defiance and persecution in the next three years than anyone in the history of the world. He would heal people, only to be accused of breaking the law. He would teach the truth about God, only to be condemned for blasphemy. He would give life to others, only to have His own life taken on the cross.

The Lord told Joseph to name Mary's child Jesus. The name literally means salvation, and God said that Jesus would save His people from their sins. The people certainly did sin, and we are still sinning today. Jesus certainly did save, and He is still saving today.

God gave Joseph a wonderful promise that Jesus would bring salvation. Joseph found peace in that promise. He found peace even though Mary was pregnant. He found peace even though he had to escape to Egypt. He found peace returning to his homeland.

God's promise was not for Joseph alone. God promised that Jesus would save His people from their sins. That includes all people who are called by His name. The peace that Joseph knew is available to all who accept God's invitation to become His children. The peace that Joseph knew is available to us today.

Accept God's invitation. Embrace his promise of salvation. Journey to the foot of the cross knowing the peace in the promise of salvation that Joseph received for all of us.

Faithful, powerful, loving Lord, I praise you for your name which means salvation. Thank you for your invitation to be called by your name and to be one of your people. I humbly accept your invitation to receive the salvation that you offer so freely to me. Watch over my every step. Make me ever grateful for your grace. Give me faith to live in your peace. In your holy name I pray, Amen.

Overcoming Every Challenge

The palms are behind us and the passion is before us. The devotions this week focus on Christ and His victory on Easter.

Challenge of Hunger

And when the tempter came to him, he said, If you are the Son of God, command that these stones be made bread. Matthew 4:3

After Christ submitted himself to be baptized in the Jordan River, he fasted for forty days. During that time, he prayed and prepared for a whole new phase of ministry. He left the comforts of home and walked through wilderness around the Jordan, a region that can be harsh and unforgiving.

Christ was human. He had human needs. Hunger is one of them. Christ is also God. He has divine powers. Making food is one of them. Sensing an opportunity to exert some influence, Satan suggested that Jesus could use His divine powers to satisfy His human needs. Jesus refused to do it.

Keep in mind that there was nothing inherently wrong with food or eating. Christ changed water to wine at the wedding in Cana. He fed thousands of people with only a few loaves and a couple of fish. He used bread and wine as symbols when He made a new covenant with His disciples.

If wine and food are so good, what was so different about stones and bread in the desert? Why did Jesus even have a second thought about the simple act of preparing a meal for Himself? Christ provided the answer. We do not live on bread alone. We feed on the word of God. To put it another way, we are not here to gratify ourselves. We exist to worship God.

87

We have come to the final week of our pilgrim journey. As we anticipate the holy day of Easter and prepare for the sacramental meal of bread and wine that we will share to celebrate the resurrection of our blessed Savior, let us remain mindful of our deep, spiritual need. Food nourishes the body, but the word of God gives life to the soul.

Holy God and giver of life, thank you for your word that feeds my soul. If my body hungers, let it remind me of my spiritual need. If my body is nourished, let it remind me that you give my soul strength. Let me always remember that as your child, I am not here to gratify myself. I am here to worship and serve you. Feed my spirit when I feed your children. Comfort my soul when I comfort them. And when I am in need, let me gratefully receive your blessings and your care. Amen.

Challenge of Fame

Then the devil took him up into the holy city, and set him on a pinnacle of the temple, and said to him, If thou be the Son of God, cast thyself down. Matthew 4:5-6a

The Gospels tell us that Jesus was in Jerusalem frequently throughout his life on earth, beginning when He was eight days old and continuing after the resurrection. It was a busy place. Herod sat in the Jewish palace. Caiaphas, the High Priest, had a separate palace. Pontius Pilate administered his government responsibilities from Jerusalem part of the time. It was an active city, and Jesus knew it well.

Under Herod the foundations of the temple in Jerusalem were expanded. New columns were raised. New gates were constructed. It was Herod's claim to fame. The work began before Jesus was born and it continued for more than a quarter of a century after Christ's ascension. This magnificent place of worship, often called "Herod's temple," served as a cross roads between the priests and the people, the rich and the poor, the powerful and the peasants. Everyone was familiar with the temple. If something happened at Herod's temple, everyone was going to hear about it.

The devil knew that Jesus had come as the good shepherd to gather His sheep. He knew that Jesus would attract followers, and this did not sit well with Satan. Instead of resisting Jesus directly, though, the devil tried to distract Jesus from His mission. Satan urged Jesus to jump from the top of Herod's temple. What a spectacle that would be! Anyone who jumped from that height and landed without a scratch would have created quite a sensation. People would notice, and people would follow. Jesus refused to jump.

Both Jesus and Satan knew that God would not let Jesus die before completing His mission. They also knew that the mission could not be completed unless Jesus followed God's plan. Satan tried to derail the mission with a temptation of fame and recognition. Jesus derailed the temptation by giving the glory and honor to God.

Completing a pilgrimage is a big undertaking and sitting at the foot of the cross is a moving experience, but we deserve no fame for it. There is nothing for us to brag about. If we do or say anything that claims credit for ourselves, then we are missing the point. The journey is for us, but it is not about us. Jesus taught us that the glory and the honor are for God alone.

God of glory, thank you for blessing me with your care and protection. Remind me with every step along this pilgrimage that although the journey is for me, it is about you. It is not about my fame or my recognition. It is about your glory and honor. Keep me strong, bear me up, and bring me safely into your loving arms. Amen.

Challenge of Power

Again, the devil took him up into an exceeding high mountain, and showed him all the kingdoms of the world, and the glory of them; and said to him, All these things will I give you, if you will fall down and worship me. Matthew 4:8-9

When Jesus was in the temple at the age of twelve, He already knew that He had a special mission from God. By the time He was thirty He would have known that His time to accomplish that mission was quickly approaching. He must have thought about this in the wilderness.

The devil had already tempted Jesus with food and fame, but Jesus showed no interest. Satan had to come up with something different. This time, the devil offered power. He offered control over kings and kingdoms. He offered the authority and the resources to carry out any mission that Jesus wanted to accomplish. But there was a catch. This time Jesus would owe something in exchange. Jesus would have to worship Satan.

The other temptations had no strings attached. They didn't need any. They would have accomplished the devil's objectives all by themselves. Each of them would have put Jesus off track because He would have served or honored Himself instead of God. This temptation had to be different, because the ruler of earthly kingdoms can give the glory to God. Satan needed Jesus to dishonor God. Jesus refused.

In reality, the power that Satan offered was only an illusion. It came on condition of worshipping Satan, and that condition only gave Jesus the power to become the devil's slave. Instead of grabbing at an illusion of instant power, Jesus began a three-year trek to Easter.

Do we prayerfully consider gifts that are offered to us? Even though a gift seems to give us the ability to do great things, if it comes on the condition that we deny the glory to God, then it is no gift at all. It is a trap. It is a sin. It takes us down the wrong path. Follow the right path. Follow Jesus' path. Follow the path that glorifies God.

Mighty God, you are the true source of all power and strength. Your words create the universe. Your breath gives life. Thank you for the choices you have placed before me. You have given me the power to glorify you. Give me the vision and the wisdom to use that power well. Let me glorify you in all that I say and do. For Thine is the kingdom, and the power, and the glory forever. Amen.

Challenge of Priests

And they that had laid hold on Jesus led him away to Caiaphas the high priest, where the scribes and the elders were assembled.
Matthew 26:57

Jesus was no stranger to the temple or to the priests. Jesus and His family visited the temple regularly when He was growing up. In addition, He had relatives at the temple. Recall that when Gabriel first told Mary that her child would be the Son of the Most High, he also told her that her relative Elizabeth would bear a son, John the Baptist. Elizabeth's husband Zechariah was a priest at the temple.

Caiaphas, the high priest, was not a new comer to the scene, either. He had been appointed by the Roman governor more than a decade before the time of Jesus' arrest. His father-in-law had been high priest before him. He was the leader of Jewish worship and custom, and he was a government insider. He was an integral and influential member in the social and political fabric of Jerusalem, and his authority was on a collision course with Jesus' mission.

Jesus and the disciples were in Jerusalem for the Passover. The Last Supper was a part of their Passover observance. During this holy religious season Caiaphas launched a plan. One night, he sent armed people to take Jesus into custody, and he assembled the scribes and the elders to conduct a trial. It was a peculiar situation, and Jesus pointed it out. "Have you come out as against a thief with swords and staves to take me? I sat daily with you teaching in the temple, and you laid no hold on me."

When Jesus was taken to Caiaphas, the challenge came to a head. This was nothing like Nicodemus who asked honest questions to learn about Jesus. It was unlike the sneaky questions about marriage, death, and taxes that were raised in an effort to trick and discredit Jesus. This was an openly hostile confrontation. The objective was clear. Jesus' life was at stake.

The Gospel record of the questioning is brief. The testimony of witnesses could not convict Jesus of anything. Their stories were so inconsistent that none could be believed. Rather than dismissing the matter and releasing Jesus, Caiaphas asked Jesus if He was the Messiah. When Jesus answered, Caiaphas believed he had won. He demanded Jesus' death. Jesus had the perfect response. He offered His life. He offered us grace.

As our path draws close to the terrible and wonderful cross, remember that Jesus faced unfair challenges. He knew the people and the politics of religion, but He faced them with confidence. He faced them with truth. He answered His call so that we can know grace. Whatever challenges we might face, Jesus is our example. No matter the cost, our calling is clear. Share the grace. Share the grace.

Eternal God, thank you for sending Jesus to be my High Priest. Thank you for letting me know Him. Thank you for letting me know You. Thank you for your courage and your honesty, your love and your grace. Give me the courage to share your love. Give me the desire to share your grace. In the name of your holy son, Jesus, the Messiah. Amen.

Challenge of Kings

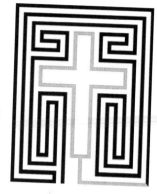

We have no king but Caesar.
John 19:15c

In the days of the judges, the people of Israel saw that other people in the region followed and served kings. The Israelites were scared that without a king as their leader, their enemies might be able to conquer them and take their land. They asked Samuel, the last of the judges, to appoint a king. This upset Samuel, but God told him not to worry. The people had not rejected Samuel as their leader. They had rejected God Himself.

More than 1,000 years later Jesus stood before Pilate, Caesar's governor in Judea. The Jews sought Jesus' death for blasphemy against God, but this was not an offense under Roman law, much less a capital offense. Another charge was needed. Jesus' accusers said that Jesus claimed to be a king. They took Christ before King Herod on these charges, too, where He was accused, ridiculed, and mocked before being handed back to Pilate.

Neither Pilate nor Herod found any cause to condemn Jesus. Even so, Jesus Christ, the King of kings and Lord of lords, was sentenced to an earthly death under the authority of earthly kings. Pilate challenged the accusers, asking if they really wanted their king to be crucified. They responded, "We have no king but Caesar." Like the Israelites from Samuel's time, they were rejecting God and clamoring for an earthly king.

Jesus was stripped, beaten, mocked, and slowly executed. Above His head a sign was posted, "King of the Jews." It was written in three languages so that everyone would know what it said. The dying, tortured form of the Savior was publicly displayed on a cross as a warning to anyone who would dare to challenge the authority and power of Caesar, the king of the world.

Incredibly, Jesus faced even this challenge with courage and unyielding faith. Many of the words that he cried from the cross can be found in the book of Psalms. A thief asked Jesus to remember him, and Christ replied, "Today you will be with me in paradise." Jesus knew who He was. He knew His purpose. He loved us so much that He endured everything to save us. He endured everything so that He could conquer everything.

Do we accept God's leadership, or do we seek earthly kings? If challenged, do we have the courage to declare that we have no king but God?

Eternal, mighty God, you are the King of kings. I stand shocked and amazed that mankind would challenge your authority—that I would challenge your authority. I am ashamed that we would ignore your love—that I would ignore your love. Thank you for your sacrifice. Thank you for your awesome power. Thank you for your grace, for I know that it is only by your power and your grace that I have hope. Amen.

Challenge of Death

Jesus, when he had cried again with a loud voice, yielded up the ghost. Matthew 27:50

And when Jesus had cried with a loud voice, he said, Father, into thy hands I commend my spirit: and having said thus, he gave up the ghost. Luke 23:46

When Jesus therefore had received the vinegar, he said, It is finished: and he bowed his head, and gave up the ghost. John 19:30

During His lifetime Jesus faced every challenge that a person can face. At His birth He faced the woes of need and deprivation, being born in a barn among animals. Yet the angels sang and shepherds worshipped. A short time later, a maniacal king ordered the death of every newborn child in an effort to kill Jesus. Yet wise men brought gifts and Jesus' family escaped to safety. He was fully human and experienced every awkward phase of growing up. Yet he grew in favor before God and before men.

Throughout His life He knew that He had a special calling. Yet He had the patience to wait until God's time had come. During His ministry some people yelled at Him and others tried to stone Him, but others were healed. Even more were fed. He was convicted and sentenced to die even though He had committed no crime. His closest followers ran for their lives. Some denied that they even knew Him.

Yet even as He hung on a cross He inspired a thief to repent.

Jesus died. Yet it was He who declared that it was finished. A Roman soldier felt compelled to declare that He was the Son of God. A righteous man sought the opportunity to bury Him. Pilate was moved to grant the request.

Although He was fully God and could have done anything that He willed, Jesus did not even attempt to escape death. He was fully human, and He completed a fully human life. All the way to the grave.

When Jesus foretold His resurrection, He knew that death and suffering had to come first. The humiliation was real. The beatings were painful. The crucifixion was agonizing. Jesus had to watch His mother suffer at His feet. He had to see the fear in His disciples' faces and the hatred in His enemies' eyes. On top of this, He carried the sins of all people for all time. Every single sin, even though He was pure and perfect and righteous. For Christ, death was not simply an event. It was another challenge, and He faced it for us. On Saturday we remember that Jesus lay in the grave. We remember that He had waited for this day. We remember that He was still waiting for resurrection. And we are waiting with Him.

It was almost time for the resurrection when Christ lay in the grave, but He waited for God's time to rise on Easter morning. We have almost reached the destination on our pilgrim journey. The journey has been long. The effort has been great. The miracle is about to happen. But we will follow our Lord's example. We will wait for God's time.

God of eternity, your word tells us that a day is as a thousand years, and a thousand years are as a day. I have a sense of eternity as I consider the body of Jesus lying in the grave. I know that His pain was real, and I know that His death was real. I know that He suffered for me. You suffered for me. Give me patience to wait for your resurrection. Give me strength to endure so that I can follow your path and do your will in your time. In the name of your holy Son, my Savior. Amen.

Victory of Life

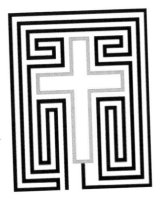

And the angel answered and said to the women, Fear not: for I know that you seek Jesus, which was crucified. He is not here: for he is risen, as he said. Come, see the place where the Lord lay.
Matthew 28:5-6

When Jesus rose from the grave He completed a mission to provide salvation to a world filled with sin and death. God had never made a secret about this mission. He had provided the model for reconciliation through the law. Everything that Jesus did had been prophesied centuries earlier. The place of His birth was foretold, His ancestry was predicted, His ministry was described, and His death and resurrection were planned. Jesus came to provide the final, perfect atonement for sin, and that is exactly what He did.

Jesus had not tried to keep His mission a secret, either. He responded to John the Baptist by recounting the ministry that He was spreading. He told His disciples that He would have to suffer. He even told them that He would be crucified. He said that He would rise again.

Even with the benefit of prophecies, scriptures, and personal contact with Jesus, though, His followers could not comprehend what was happening. The idea that God incarnate had lived and walked on earth was impossible to understand, especially when Jesus had been executed. Death on the cross seemed so final. The shock and terror of that event had overwhelmed them to the point that any understanding that they might have had about the resurrection had been replaced with anguish and fear.

The women at the tomb did not expect the resurrection. Neither did the disciples. The Lord appeared to travelers on the road to Emmaus and walked with them. They were so fixated on the crucifixion that they could not recognize the risen Savior. Thomas would not believe the other disciples' account of Christ's return. He had to experience it for himself.

In the face of fear and confusion among His friends and followers, Jesus used a familiar, loving voice to help Mary recognize Him. When He appeared to His disciples, He said, "Peace." At the tomb He left His angels as messengers to announce the resurrection concisely but gently. The nightmare of death was over. The victory of life was proclaimed.

Our journey into the labyrinth is complete. We have considered many scriptures and lessons along the path. We have prayed and meditated so that we can be prepared to experience God in a new and special way. Enjoy this time with the Creator. At the same time, remember that we are mere disciples, too. Just as the disciples failed to comprehend the resurrection on that first Easter morning, we are limited in our ability to understand God's work in the world today. Here, in the center of the labyrinth, at the foot of the cross, listen for Jesus' familiar, loving voice. Know that His desire for you is peace. Accept the message of Easter. Death has died. Life is victorious.

God of life, I praise you, and I thank you for this journey that has brought me to the foot of the cross. You have conquered death and given me hope of new life with you. I have come to commune with you and to live in you. Speak to me. Tell me of your love. Give to me your peace. In your gentle kindness, give me the deep assurance that eternal life is mine. Death has died. Life is victorious. You are victorious. And I am in you. In the name of your glorious, risen Son, my Lord and my Savior, Jesus Christ, Amen.

Index

Made in the USA
Lexington, KY
17 February 2010